THE NATURE LIBRARY

BABY ANIMALS

DAVID ALDERTON

CRESCENT BOOKS

NEW YORK

CLB 2584

This 1991 edition published by Crescent Books,
distributed by Outlet Book Company, Inc.,
a Random House Company, 225 Park Avenue South,
New York, New York 10003.

Printed and bound in Hong Kong

ISBN 0-517-05155-9

8 7 6 5 4 3 2 1

Library of Congress Cataloging-in-Publication Data
Baby animals
        p. cm – (Nature Library)
    Includes index.
    Summary: Looks at a wide range of baby animals and examines how they
grow and are equipped to survive.
    ISBN 0-517-05155-9 : $6.99
    1. Animals – Infancy – Juvenile literature. (1. Animals – Infancy.) I. Series.
QL763.B34 1991   90-41152
591.56 – dc20   CIP
                                                                        AC

Credits

Edited and designed: Ideas into Print, Vera Rogers and Stuart Watkinson
Picture Editors: Annette Lerner, John Kaprielian
Photographs: Photo Researchers Inc., New York
Commissioning Editor: Andrew Preston
Production: Ruth Arthur, Sally Connolly, David Proffit, Andrew Whitelaw
Director of Production: Gerald Hughes
Director of Publishing: David Gibbon
Typesetting: SX Composing Ltd.
Color separations: Scantrans Pte. Ltd., Singapore

The Author

David Alderton has had a life-long interest in wildlife. Since graduating
from Cambridge University, his work as a specialist writer on animals has
enabled him to travel far afield, observing many creatures in their natural
habitats. David also attends various international meetings where
conservation matters are discussed, and he is acutely aware of the
difficulties faced by many species today in their constant battle for survival.

CONTENTS

Above: Ducklings hold a special fascination, here photographed at a park in Arizona. Many ornamental breeds have been developed, delighting visitors to gardens throughout the world.

Left: Young gentoo penguins huddle together on the subantarctic island of South Georgia. All the world's penguins live in the Southern Hemisphere, where some species face severe weather conditions during part of the year. The breeding cycle is closely keyed into the turn of the seasons, so that the chicks stand the best chance of survival.

BUTTERFLIES – A REMARKABLE TRANSFORMATION

Over 20,000 different types of butterfly have already been identified and new species are still being discovered. They are found in both tropical and temperate parts of the world and all have a similar life cycle, starting from a small egg. Using her sense of sight, the female butterfly first searches for a suitable plant on which to lay her eggs. Once she has spotted a likely leaf, she alights upon it for a closer examination. Her final decision will be influenced by a variety of considerations, such as its position relative to sunlight, whether other eggs are present or if the leaf is tough enough. These factors are important in ensuring that the eggs hatch and the emerging caterpillars survive.

Caterpillars – the larval stage in the life cycle – feed exclusively on vegetation. Some can safely eat highly poisonous plants, such as cycads (primitive plants that resemble ferns). This diet protects the caterpillars, because the toxins originally contained in the plants will, in turn, harm any predators that eat the caterpillars. These 'toxic' caterpillars are often brightly coloured, warning birds and other creatures that they are potentially harmful.

As the caterpillars grow, they shed their skins until they are ready to pupate. They then seek out a sheltered spot, where they can weave their cocoons

and turn into a pupa – often called a chrysalis. At this stage, they rely mainly on camouflage to conceal their presence, but a few species have highly colourful pupae which, like the caterpillars, are poisonous.

Within the pupa, the caterpillar changes dramatically in appearance and finally emerges as an adult butterfly, relying mainly on nectar from flowers to sustain it during its brief lifespan. Soon after breeding, most butterflies will die, although a few do hibernate during the winter and emerge in spring.

Below: Monarch butterfly eggs on milkweed. Certain chemicals in milkweed affect the hearts of vertebrates and these chemicals can be passed from caterpillar to the adult butterfly, protecting the adult against predators.

Right: A monarch caterpillar poised to pupate. The bright coloration of this larva warns of its toxic effects. It is further protected by the presence of pairs of antennae at both ends of its body, designed to confuse a predator. The longer pair are located on the larva's head.

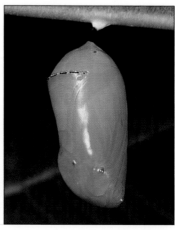

Above: Butterflies have different types of pupae. This monarch pupa has anchored itself using the hook or 'cremaster' at its rear end to grip onto a silk pad attaching to a leaf. Although this might appear a relatively inert stage in the life cycle, dramatic changes are taking place.

Left: Many butterflies have a limited distribution. This species, found on the Caribbean island of Trinidad, is called the '89' butterfly, because of the unusual patterning on the underside of the wing, clearly evident here.

Above: The striking eyespots create a fearsome appearance. This larva rears up like a snake.

Right: The adult spicebush swallowtail, with its larva above. A North American species.

Left: Butterflies are active in the day. They can be distinguished from moths by their brighter coloration and by the knobbed tip to each of their antennae.

Right: Swallowtail butterflies have a pointed extension on the rear of each wing. In some areas, caterpillars feed on citrus plants, causing major damage.

Above: This pupa will soon be hatching into an adult monarch butterfly. The breeding habits of this species vary throughout its wide range, which extends from southern Canada as far as Paraguay in South America. They are strongly influenced by local temperatures.

Left: A lovely monarch butterfly emerges. In a few moments its wings will inflate, enabling it to fly. These butterflies can travel up to 125km (78miles) in a single day. When migrating, some cover distances of 2,500km(1,562miles).

Above: The monarch butterfly expanded its range greatly during the last century, and now breeds as far north as Canada. In the autumn it returns to warmer climes along the coast of California and in the Mexican state of Michoacan, where it hibernates in vast numbers.

CICHLIDS – CARING AND ATTENTIVE PARENTS

These fish are found in Central and South America, as well as in Africa, and two species are also present in Asia. Males are highly territorial, especially when in breeding condition, and will drive away other males that attempt to encroach on their territory. Initially, females may also be attacked but, assuming they are in breeding condition, this behaviour soon switches to courtship, which may entail the fishes locking mouths and wrestling with each other. Some cichlids dig a shallow pit in which to lay and fertilize their eggs, whereas others clean an area of rockwork or a small underwater cave in preparation for their eggs, which adhere to the site.

The most remarkable species are probably the mouthbrooding cichlids. The eggs are fertilized by the male after they have left the female's body. His anal fin, situated close to the vent, is marked with dots that closely resemble the eggs. When the female has finished laying her eggs, she scoops them into her mouth and also tries to gather in the egglike spots on the male's anal fin. This stimulates the male into releasing his semen, or milt, from just behind the fin, thus ensuring that all the eggs in the female's mouth are fertilized. Depending on the species, this may be the sole method of fertilization, but sometimes the male quickly fertilizes the eggs before they are retrieved by the female. In this case, when the female ingests the milt, she ensures that all the eggs are fertilized, including any that were missed before.

Above: A female Salvin's cichlid. It is found in Central America.

Cichlids are noted for the close attention that the parents give to their eggs and fry. In mouthbrooding species, the female retains the eggs in her mouth until they hatch. Hatching can take nearly two weeks and the female probably does not feed during this time. Even when she has finally released the fry, they will dart back inside her mouth if danger threatens.

Left: Water conditions, notably the relative balance of acidity or alkalinity, may influence the sex of *Cichlasoma* cichlid fry.

Above: Salvin's cichlids can be highly aggressive towards other fish that venture too close to their offspring. Their bright coloration intensifies when they are breeding and may serve as a warning to potential predators.

Below: The shape of the rear of the dorsal fin on the back distinguishes this male *Cichlasoma nigrofasciata* from the female (left).

Left: These dwarf African cichlids normally seek out dark caves for spawning. When they breed in aquarium surroundings, their eggs must be protected from the light, otherwise they are unlikely to hatch. There is a strong pair bond between a breeding pair. The female watches over the eggs, fanning them with her tail, while the male drives off potential intruders.

Right: Fry from a successful spawning. Parental care increases the likelihood of fry surviving the early period of life.

Below: The fry will eat a host of small invertebrates, and feed frequently throughout the day. Young cichlids remain under the watchful eye of their parents for up to two months; some will grow faster than others.

Below: The discus is one of the most spectacular of all cichlids and, understandably, a very popular aquarium fish. The parents lay their eggs on submerged rock or wood.

Right: It takes a couple of days for the eggs to hatch, and a similar period before the fry are free-swimming. They then feed on a special mucus secretion, produced on the adults' skin.

POISON ARROW FROGS – BEAUTIFUL BUT DEADLY

These brightly coloured little amphibians are found in areas of Central and South America. Their skin glands produce a powerful poison that is used by the native Indians to tip their arrows. When the toxin enters the bloodstream, it causes muscular paralysis, and one frog can produce enough poison for 40 arrows!

Each male poison arrow frog has his own territory and he will fertilize the eggs of breeding females that enter this area. The female does not lay her eggs in water, but in a damp spot on the forest floor. She produces far fewer eggs than most frogs, often laying clutches of less than ten at a time. Once the eggs are laid, the female leaves them with the male, who fertilizes them and ensures that they remain moist.

Depending on the species, one or both parents remain close to the eggs until they hatch after about ten days. When the tadpoles emerge, their parents transport them, often individually, to water. Each tadpole hitches a ride on the frog's back, and is usually deposited in the cup of a bromeliad plant, where water collects. Here, the female feeds her offspring, even using unfertilized eggs. Studies have shown that when the female approaches a tadpole, it 'begs' for food, causing her to release eggs for the tadpole to eat.

This unique method of parental care continues for nearly three months, until the tadpole has metamorphosed into a young frog. It then hops out of the bromeliad plant and starts to feed on small insects. Youngsters take about a year to mature before they reproduce. Unlike frogs from more temperate climates, poison arrow frogs can breed at any time of year.

Left: Poison arrow frogs occur in tropical areas, where there may be little free-standing water. They carry their tadpoles in a mucus membrane on their back.

Below: Because they care for their fry, there is less need for these frogs to produce large numbers of offspring to maintain their population. Apart from people, they face few predators, but deforestation threatens local populations.

Above: The bright coloration of poison arrow frogs serves to convey a stark warning of their deadly nature to likely predators.

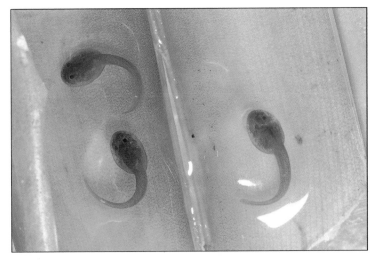

Left: Young poison arrow frog tadpoles. At this stage, they are dependent on their parents to move them to water, where they can complete the change from larval form to young frogs by the process of metamorphosis.

Right: The hind legs are the first pair of limbs to grow, but at this stage they are only used for swimming, rather than walking on land. Inside the body, other significant changes are taking place. The gills that enable the tadpoles to breathe in water are to be replaced by lungs.

Right: The adult frog, following its metamorphosis. Individual markings on poison arrow frogs can differ quite widely. It is estimated that there are at least 118 different species.

Below: This young poison arrow frog is almost ready to leave the water. Both pairs of legs are well developed, and the tail is much shorter, as it is being resorbed into the body. The frogs then spend most of their life on land.

Left: New species of poison arrow frog are still being discovered, and there is much to learn about the differences between them. These frogs are usually described by their scientific names.

Right: The so-called dendrobatid and phyllobatid groups are the most colourful poison arrow frogs. They range in size from 15-50mm(0.6-2in). This dendrobatid species was photographed in the Canaima National Park, Venezuela.

GREEN TURTLES – RUNNING THE GAUNTLET TO THE SEA

The green turtle is found throughout the world's tropical oceans. They browse mainly on plants, such as seaweeds. It takes over 20 years for young turtles to reach maturity and, after mating at sea, the females head back to the beaches where they themselves were hatched. No-one knows how they find their way back after so long; it may be that young females, returning to nest for the first time, follow older individuals back to the breeding grounds, since it seems unlikely that they could recall the way on their own.

In water, the turtle is an agile swimmer, but as it leaves the sea to climb onto the beach, its flippers are of little use and it has to drag itself over the sand. Turtles normally come ashore to lay their eggs under cover of darkness, so that they are less vulnerable to predators. Having scooped out a nesting chamber with their flippers, they lay over 100 eggs in rapid succession. The eggs are coated in mucus, so that they will not break as they tumble into the hollow. Then the female turtle carefully brushes the sand back over the eggs and heads out to sea. It may be two or three years before she returns to lay again.

The heat of the sun is sufficient for the eggs to develop and also influences the sex of the offspring, higher temperatures producing a greater proportion of females. When they are due to hatch, about seven weeks later, the small turtles scramble out of their eggshells and dig their way to the surface. Large numbers of eggs hatch at the same time so that at least some have a chance of surviving the countless predators, from gulls to crabs, that decimate the hatchlings as they strive to reach the sea. Probably less than one hatchling in a thousand will attain maturity.

Below: Males use their powerful jaws to inflict painful bites on females during courtship. Divers may be mistakenly attacked in some cases.

Above: An adult turtle with a newly hatched baby heading to the sea. Turtles show no parental care and hatchlings may be crushed by adults coming ashore to lay more eggs.

Below: Relatively few hatchlings survive to reach the sea. Those that do, swim quickly away from the beach, pausing when they encounter a suitable mat of floating vegetation. Then they rest and start to feed.

Above: Turtles lay relatively large numbers of eggs. Many fail to hatch, however, being destroyed by predators before the end of the incubation period.

Left: A nesting female on Floreana Island, part of the Galapagos group off the coast of Ecuador. Turtles often lay eggs under cover of darkness.

Left: A young green turtle has a potential lifespan of perhaps 50 years or more. During its life, it may swim vast distances. Tagging has shown that these turtles may cross the Atlantic Ocean, covering at least 5,950km(3,700miles). They can cruise at about 7.4kph(4.6mph), and may even reach speeds of 36kph (22.4mph) if threatened.

Above: A baby turtle struggles to the surface from its nest above the upper tide mark.

Above: A group of hatchlings will instinctively head for the sea. It may be the sound of the waves that attracts them here, since turtles have poor eyesight. At first, they survive on the remains of their yolk sacs.

Right: The mad scamper to the sea is fraught with danger. Conservation efforts have been directed towards hatching turtle eggs artificially and returning the hatchlings to the ocean, thus eliminating this vulnerable stage.

SNAKES – TWO WAYS TO ENSURE BREEDING SUCCESS

About 2,700 different types of snakes are known and whereas many species lay eggs, a few give birth to live young. Snakes that produce eggs are the more prolific group, because they lay more eggs to compensate for those likely to be destroyed before hatching. Live-born snakes have a greater chance of survival; if they are poisonous, they can immediately defend themselves, and they can move to escape possible predators.

Pythons are the best-known group of egglaying snakes. These large snakes are found exclusively in tropical regions of Africa and Australia. They often grow to over 6m(20ft) long and kill by constriction, wrapping their body around their prey until it suffocates. When mating, the male python entwines himself around the female, using vestigial limbs, known as spurs, located on either side of his genital opening. If she is not immediately ready to mate, she may rear up. If the female is cooperative, however, she positions her body so that the male and female genital openings are in close contact, enabling penetration to take place. Fertilization occurs internally and, after mating, the pair split up and go their separate ways. Large snakes, such as pythons, are relatively sluggish by nature and not seriously inconvenienced by the bulk of the eggs inside their bodies. Smaller fast-moving snakes, such as the rough green snakes are likely to be at a disadvantage, however, because the extra weight handicaps their hunting skills. Giving birth to live young has also enabled snakes to move into parts of the world where they might otherwise not survive, because the external temperature is too low to guarantee that eggs would hatch. Species that live in water, such as many sea snakes, also often give birth to live young. This saves them having to leave their aquatic environment to move onto land, where they are relatively helpless and vulnerable.

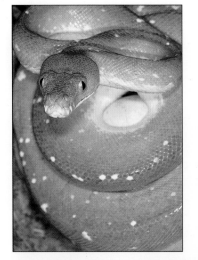

Left: A female green tree python with her eggs. About three or four months after mating, she will lay up to 100 eggs, all with leathery skins. She curls her body around them and her body warmth, acquired from basking in the sun, is sufficient to ensure embryo development. Her body muscles may twitch at fairly regular intervals; this may slightly raise the temperature of the eggs. Although females may occasionally leave their nest site during this period to drink or slough their skin, they never venture far away.

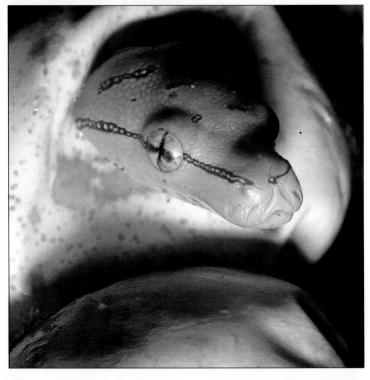

Left: Young snakes grow rapidly, with pythons often trebling their length within a year of hatching. As they grow, they shed their skin regularly. This is an eastern sand viper, a poisonous species, beginning to slough its skin. Females give birth to live young.

Above: A young green tree python emerges from its egg. It is yellow at first, but will start to change to the predominantly green colour of adults when it is six months old. Hatching may take about 10 weeks and once the youngsters start to emerge from the eggs, their mother takes no further interest in them. In the trees, these pythons hunt for birds, rodents and bats.

Above: By the time the young are ready to emerge, the eggs have grown noticeably, being broader than the adult snake.

Above: The rough green snake is a narrow-bodied species found largely in the eastern United States. It feeds mainly on invertebrates and lays about a dozen eggs. These expand in diameter as the embryos grow.

Right: Newly hatched rough green snakes are about 20cm (8in) long and may grow to 100cm(39in). They soon head for warm locations to bask. Even the heat of a human hand can raise their body temperature.

Left: A female Baird's ratsnake lays her eggs. These snakes are closely related to the Texas ratsnake and are found in southern central parts of the state. The patterning of this group of ratsnakes alters as the hatchlings grow, except in the case of the grey ratsnake.

ALLIGATORS – NEST-BUILDING REPTILES

As spring advances and the water temperature starts to rise, alligators begin to show signs of breeding behaviour. Males display to their intended mates by head-slapping – crashing their heads down onto the water – and both sexes roar loudly. After mating has taken place in the water, with the largest females and males mating together first, each female seeks out a suitable nesting site for her eggs. It is vital that she chooses a site that cannot be flooded, because immersion under water for more than 12 hours will be fatal to the embryos developing inside the eggs.

The female alligator usually builds her nest close to the shore on a bank, and may return to an area she has used before. First she clears the ground, breaking off pieces of vegetation or pulling them up in her teeth and then piling them up in the centre of the site. The female continues to add more twigs, leaves and mud, until the mound may be as much as 2m(78in) in diameter and 71cm(28in) high. During this stage, she repeatedly crawls on top of the mound to crush the material down, before digging a chamber about

30cm(12in) deep at the top. Eventually, in the space of little more than 30 minutes, she lays up to 50 eggs in the hollow and finally covers the nesting chamber.

Throughout the incubation period, which lasts about 65 days, the female remains near the nest. During this time, she may attack raccoons and other predators that venture too close. When she hears the calls of the young alligators from within, the female alligator breaks open the mound and carefully helps her offspring out of their eggs, rolling these in her mouth to crack the shell if necessary. Then she carries the youngsters down to the water and the group, known as a pod, remains together, sometimes right through the year until the following spring.

Above: An opened nest of alligator eggs. Research has confirmed that the incubation temperature has a controlling influence on the sex of the hatchlings. This was first noted in American alligators in 1982, and has since been confirmed in other species of crocodilian.

Left: The female alligator builds a bulky nest of vegetation in which she lays her eggs. In many cases, she will remain nearby, helping the young to hatch. In the reptilian world, such a degree of parental care is unique to crocodilians. Chinese alligators nest in similar fashion.

Left: Juvenile alligators sunning themselves in the Corkscrew Swamp Sanctuary, Florida. This species was extensively hunted and its skin used for leather. Now it is protected and numbers have increased.

Below: At first, alligators eat small prey, such as insects, and then progress to bigger quarry, including fish and turtles. They are strictly carnivorous in their feeding habits, but rarely present any danger to people.

Right: Young alligators emerge in late summer and their mother assists them to water and watches over them here. Their initial bright coloration serves as disruptive camouflage, helping to conceal their presence in the water. Alligator hatchlings measure just 23cm(9in), but they can grow to over 5.6m(19ft) long. Their life expectancy is well over half a century, assuming they can survive the critical early years, during which cannibalism is a real danger.

Above: Surrounded by duckweed, this young alligator remains largely hidden. Its eyes are positioned high on the head for good visibility. Growth rate depends on the temperature of its surroundings, which affects feeding behaviour. Studies show that alligators in the warmer, southern part of their range develop the fastest.

Left: Sexual maturity in these reptiles is related to size, rather than age. Males tend to grow more quickly, reaching maturity at a body length of about 1.8m (6ft). Southerly populations can mature at only seven years old, but it may take double this time further north. Alligators will hibernate to avoid the worst of the winter weather.

Right: Apart from hunters, adult alligators face few threats, although increasing human contact has brought problems. Lumbering across roads, a number of these reptiles are killed in collisions with vehicles every year, and pollution of the waterways poses an increasing threat to young and old alligators alike.

DUCKLINGS – A SURE SIGN OF SPRING

Fluffy baby ducklings are an unmistakable sign of spring. There are many different types of duck, with ornamental breeds such as the mandarin being kept for their superb coloration. The so-called domestic ducks are variants of these ornamental forms, which have been developed over the years for their eggs and as table birds. They tend to be less colourful.

Ducks nest close to the water, with some, such as the Carolina, preferring to lay their eggs in suitable tree hollows rather than on the ground. Here, they should be safer from predators such as foxes. The eggs take 25-30 days to hatch, depending on the type of duck. The ducklings will then follow their mother into the water and soon start using their beaks to search for food, which often includes the water plant appropriately called duckweed. She does not actually feed them directly at any stage, but they learn to follow her example as to what is edible.

Although there may be eight or ten ducklings at the outset, their numbers are soon likely to be reduced by predators. Other birds such as herons prey on these young birds and, out of sight in the water, large fish such as pike may seize them from below.

When they first hatch, ducklings are unable to fly, but their flight feathers develop as their down is replaced by adult plumage. In many cases, drakes and ducks look alike for part of the year, but then, just before the breeding season, the drakes moult into more colourful feathers. At this time, drakes can become aggressive in the search for a mate.

Right: Many ducks breed on the ground, but a few nest in hollow trees. Chicks jump down onto the ground.

Right: A one-month old mallard duckling.

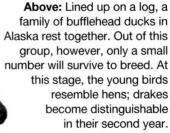

Above: Lined up on a log, a family of bufflehead ducks in Alaska rest together. Out of this group, however, only a small number will survive to breed. At this stage, the young birds resemble hens; drakes become distinguishable in their second year.

Right: On Isle Bicquette, in Quebec, Canada, an eider duck hatches from its egg. Eider ducks are mainly found in coastal areas. Ducklings feed on shrimps and other small marine creatures. Down feathers have been harvested for centuries as eiderdown.

Left: Baby ducklings hatch as miniature adults, with fluffy plumage. They may head for water almost immediately, but have little defence against danger until their flight feathers are sufficiently developed.

Above: A female mallard with her ducklings. On land, they are vulnerable to foxes and other mammalian predators, but even when swimming, they risk hidden dangers, and may be seized from below by large fish.

Left: These baby North American red-head ducklings are closely related to the European pochard. In winter, the youngsters fly south, as far as central Mexico, to escape the worst of the harsh weather.

Below: Wandering across a salt marsh mudflat, a female mallard and her family search for food. These ducks often retreat to salt water areas in winter, when inland waters become frozen. They feed on aquatic vegetation.

HUMMINGBIRDS – BRIGHT JEWELS OF THE AIR

There are over 300 species of hummingbird, most of which live in tropical areas of America, although some species extend into North America up to Canada, while others are found southwards towards Chile. Male hummingbirds are normally brightly coloured, with highly iridescent plumage that they use to display to their intended mates. They are also surprisingly aggressive, and will fiercely defend their territory.

Once mating has occurred, the hen is left on her own to arrange the nest. She chooses a secluded spot, often at a fork in a branch, and uses mosses and spider webs to prepare a deep, well-camouflaged cup-shaped nest for the two white eggs.

Hummingbirds lay the smallest eggs of any birds; those of the Vervain hummingbird from Jamaica, for example, measure less than 1cm(0.4in) long and weigh just 0.365gm(0.0129oz). The incubation period lasts 14-19 days, depending on the species, and the tiny young are blind and helpless when they hatch. At this stage, the female catches countless tiny insects, which she feeds to her offspring. Hovering near the nest, she carefully positions her beak within the begging mouths of the chicks and regurgitates the food.

Youngsters develop quite slowly, with the rearing period lasting about three weeks on average. However, once they leave the nest, the young hummingbirds are completely feathered and almost as agile in flight as their parents. They can beat their wings faster than any other bird, with a rate of no less than 55 beats per second when they are hovering in flight.

Below: Rufous-tailed hummingbird chicks. Hummingbirds generally lay two eggs, with an interval of 48 hours between them. In most cases, the nest is cup-shaped, as shown here.

Below: Incubation only begins once the second egg is laid. The young hummingbirds are helpless at first, but grow rapidly, feeding largely on a diet of tiny insects, rather than nectar.

Left: To conserve precious energy, these tiny birds often rest on a perch at dusk, their body temperature falling dramatically. They only awake from their torpor when the temperature rises the next day.

Above: Hummingbirds that build cup-shaped nests, rather than covered pendant nests, always breed outside the rainy period. During a prolonged deluge, the nest would become flooded, and the chicks would be lost.

Left: Broad-billed hummingbirds. All hummingbirds feed on nectar, normally hovering in front of the flower and using their long tongues to extract this sweet mix of sugars. They will also catch small insects. Many species have highly iridescent plumage.

Above: Hummingbirds display a unique degree of aerial mastery. Their wing structure differs from that of most other birds, except swifts. They can rotate their wings at the shoulder joints.

Left: A young broad-tailed hummingbird prepares to leave the nest. To build up muscular strength, it will flap its wings for several days beforehand, and is then immediately able to hover.

Above: The female hummingbird is responsible for rearing the offspring, and continues to feed them for a further period once they have left the nest. She may sometimes have more than one clutch of chicks in succession.

Right: Cock hummingbirds, such as this broad-billed, are invariably more colourful than females. The bright throat patch is used as part of the mating display. They have distinctive territorial calls to deter rivals.

SEABIRDS – NESTING IN ESTABLISHED COLONIES

Seabirds can be broadly divided into two categories. Some, such as the albatrosses, spend most of their time in the sky, swooping down to the sea to feed, whereas others live mostly in direct contact with the oceans. In both cases, however, they come together in groups during the breeding period. Gannets nest in huge colonies on precarious rock faces. Bird Rock in the Gulf of St. Lawrence, Canada, for example, was home to 150,000 pairs of gannets in 1833. But when a lighthouse was built nearby in 1869, fishermen killed huge numbers of birds during the breeding season and within 30 years the colony was almost wiped out. Since then, protection has ensured that the numbers of birds nesting here has risen again.

Gannets return to the same nesting site every year, adding seaweed and other material to it each time. The hen lays a single egg, but instead of brooding it with the body, gannets use their feet. Each parent takes it in turn to incubate the egg, which hatches after six weeks. At this stage, the chick is naked and helpless, but soon acquires a covering of white down. Its parents dive for fish, sometimes to depths of 27m(90ft), swallowing their catch underwater before

returning to the nest to feed the chick by regurgitation. Huge congregations of seabirds are clearly vulnerable if the fish on which they feed decline in number.

Gannets are able to fly by about three months old. At this point, they are suddenly abandoned by their parents and must leave the ledge on which they hatched. They spend the next few weeks at sea until their wing muscles are fully developed and, having used up their store of body fat, the youngsters start to dive for food.

Above: Albatrosses also favour islands for breeding purposes. As with gannets, these birds nest in colonies. Pairs have only a single chick, as shown here.

Left: By nesting in inaccessible localities, such as cliff faces overlooking the ocean, gannets are safe from most predators. Overcrowding may occur.

Left: A cape gannet with chick, photographed on Bird Island off the coast of South Africa. Large groups of gannets prefer to nest on islands. Nine species are recognized across the world's oceans. They are quite vocal.

Right: A laysan albatross feeds its chick. Many seabirds have a slow reproductive rate and albatrosses are unlikely to breed for the first time until they are at least four years old, maybe even older. They normally pair for life, which can be 30 years or more. The birds spend their time wandering the oceans, the male albatross returning to the breeding site first, followed by the hen. Colonies sometimes consist of thousands of birds.

Below: A laysan albatross chick on Midway Atoll, an island in the Pacific to the northwest of Hawaii. During the Second World War there was an airbase here, and albatrosses nesting close to the runway represented a serious hazard to pilots taking off and landing. Known as 'bird strike', a mid-air collision with a bird can still occur and may cause a fatal crash.

Right: While it learns to fly, the young laysan albatross may end up floating in the sea. It must strengthen its wing muscles before it can glide with skill, skimming over the waves.

Below: This albatross and other seabirds face an increasingly uncertain future, threatened by oil spills, chemical dumping and intensive fishing of the oceans.

CUCKOOS – RAISED BY FOSTER PARENTS

Cuckoos are found both in tropical and temperate parts of the world. The most familiar species are those with parasitic breeding habits. Instead of bothering to build a nest and rear their own chicks, the hens of these cuckoos deposit eggs in the nests of other birds. Interestingly, this procedure is not carried out at random; on the contrary, studies have shown that cuckoos watch their intended victims closely as they start to nest, and the laying cycles of both host bird and cuckoo are synchronized.

When the chosen foster parent starts laying, the hen cuckoo waits until the nest is briefly unoccupied, flies down to remove an egg and lays her own almost at once. She may then either eat the egg that she has stolen or simply drop it some distance away from the nest. The colour of her egg closely mimics that of the others in the nest, and the cuckoo chick hatches either at the same time or even before its nestmates. Almost at once, the young cuckoo is able to muster sufficient strength to push unhatched eggs and any nestlings over the side of the nest and onto the ground.

The growth rate of the young cuckoo is enormous, and it cannot afford to tolerate any challengers to its food supply, which is constantly maintained by the foster parents. They are soon dwarfed by the intruder, but accept the cuckoo chick as their own and diligently feed it for over three weeks, until it is ready to leave the nest.

There are about 127 species of cuckoos, and in different parts of the world they parasitize different host species. Cuckoos from more temperate areas are migratory, leaving for warmer climates in the autumn when the number of insects on which they feed begins to decline. However, young birds often remain behind for longer than adults, building up their strength for the flight but, even alone, they instinctively find their way to their winter quarters.

Above: Cuckoos can be broadly divided into two groups: parasitic species lay eggs in the nests of other birds. Others, such as the black-billed cuckoo shown here, lay in the usual manner and rear their own chicks.

Left: A young common cuckoo in the nest. A newly hatched cuckoo has a special hollow in the back that enables it to roll eggs up the side of the nest, so they can be thrown out. Each female cuckoo lays only one egg in the nest of a host, but in some areas, more than one hen may lay in the same nest. The first cuckoo to hatch normally ejects the other. However, nests containing two cuckoos that finally fledged together have been recorded.

Left: The hatchling parasitic cuckoo weighs only about 4gm(0.14oz) but, remarkably, it quadruples its weight within just four days and is then equivalent to its foster parents.

Below: A hedge sparrow works hard to meet the demands of the young cuckoo. At this stage, the chick is too large to be brooded and risks chilling, especially after prolonged rainfall. It will be able to fly at three weeks old.

Above: A black-billed cuckoo feeds its chicks. The eggs of these non-parasitic species vary from white to pale green and blue, whereas the eggs of parasitic cuckoos usually resemble those of the host species. This helps to disguise them.

Below: Non-parasitic cuckoos, including this yellow-billed species, have a very short incubation, lasting only 10 days. Chicks leave the nest when just eight days old, having been fed on a diet of insects. This species migrates northwards from South America for about five months.

CHICKS – DESCENDED FROM THE JUNGLE FOWL

The ancestors of our domestic poultry are the jungle fowl of Southeast Asia. The domestication process possibly began as long ago as 4,000 BC, and jungle fowl had certainly been domesticated in India by 3,200 BC. From there they spread around the world, with such birds being valued both for their eggs and as a source of meat. Domestic fowl may retain many of the traits of their original ancestors, but in certain respects domestication has considerably altered both the appearance and characteristics of these birds. For example, strains have been developed for egg laying throughout the year, whereas in the wild, the breeding period is nowhere near as extensive.

Jungle fowl hens simply lay clutches of up to eight eggs, which take about three weeks to hatch. Although they live together in flocks for much of the year, the hens separate at this time and can prove aggressive in defence of their nest. This is usually a hollow scraping under a bush or tree. The young birds are covered in down when they hatch and are capable of running after their mother almost immediately. At this stage, they tend to feed on insects, rather than on seeds and plants.

In the modern poultry industry, hens rarely hatch their own eggs. Instead, these are removed and transferred to large incubators and the young chickens are reared on specially prepared diets, such as chick crumbs. Breeders have also produced small forms of chicken, known as bantams. These are available in a variety of colours and some have a very ornamental appearance. One particular bantam, the silkie, is particularly valued for hatching the eggs of other breeds that may be reluctant to incubate their own eggs.

Above: A wide range of poultry breeds have been bred from the jungle fowl. Some have been developed specially for egg laying, whereas others have been bred for a fast growth rate.

A third group are valued for their appearance, and include the small forms known as bantams.

Below: Chicks may differ in appearance from their mother. The greatest variety in plumage coloration is evident among the 50 or so breeds of bantam. Depending on breed, they have the most elaborate plumage.

Right: A young chick. It is able to feed itself as soon as it has hatched, but for the first day or so it uses up the yolk sac that nourished it in the egg.

Above: These chicks have been bred as broilers. They grow rapidly, reaching the required weight for market within seven weeks. Birds are kept in groups and fed throughout their lives on specially formulated diets.

Above right: Chicks are able to run as soon as they have hatched, but are at risk from the elements and can become saturated and chilled in the rain. Jungle fowl have many chicks, but most die before maturity.

Right: A mother hen broods her chicks outdoors. She alone is concerned with incubating the eggs and brooding the chicks. She will call them if danger threatens, and the chicks stay close to her after hatching.

Left: Chicks rapidly lose heat from their small bodies, in spite of their downy feathers. They will huddle together and are brooded by their mother, especially during the night.

Below: Although they appear friendly towards each other now, young cockerels become very territorial as they grow older, and fight viciously, using the spurs on their legs in combat.

SWANS – DEVOTED AND DEFENSIVE PARENTS

There are nine species of swan, which can be distinguished from other waterfowl by their particularly long necks and the flattened shape of their beaks. Adult swans of all species are either black or white, or a combination of these colours.

When they are ready to breed, these large birds construct a sizeable mound of vegetation, incorporating twigs, leaves and other debris, usually close to, or even in, shallow water. Here, the female, known as the pen, will lay five or six eggs, which she incubates alone for about 35 days. The male, called a cob, remains nearby, guarding the nest site. Males can be very aggressive at this time and it is not unusual for them to attack people, if they venture too close.

There is a strong pair bond in swans, and cob and pen mate for life. Both help to look after the young cygnets once they hatch, and may actually carry them on their backs when the young birds want to rest. The youngsters take to the water soon after hatching, in their grey downy feathering.

The family group is likely to stay together until the start of the following breeding season. It is not unusual for the swans to migrate long distances to their winter quarters in a milder locality. By flying with their parents on this journey, the young swans learn the route and will later be able to undertake this migration alone. Swans are long-lived birds, and may survive into their thirties. Youngsters are unlikely to breed for the first time until they are at least three years old.

Right: The mute swan is common on stretches of water in Europe and may even be seen in tidal areas. In the UK, they are often semi-domesticated and have been regarded as royal birds since the eleventh century.

Below: This black swan cygnet is duller than its parents. This species, found in Australia and New Zealand, is less territorial than many other swans, and it is not uncommon for pairs to nest in relatively large colonies.

Right: Cygnets enter the water shortly after hatching, but need to rest occasionally. They may climb onto their parents' back, as shown here; this method of carriage is most likely to be seen in mute swans. In spite of their common name, the young of this species do have a piping call; adults can also vocalize.

Left: All swans build a bulky nesting platform for their eggs. They often select a site on a small island, rather than at the water's edge, where they would be more at risk from predators. Swans are closely related to geese and are found on all the continents, with the notable exception of Africa.

Left: Whistling swans are able to survive in the cold northern latitudes where they occur, being protected by a dense covering of feathers. Individuals may have up to 25,216 feathers.

Below: Swans often appear rather ungainly on land and may have difficulty in taking off because of their bulk. At first, cygnets are unable to fly and they can only retreat to water.

OWLS – BEAUTIFUL BIRDS OF PREY

These distinctive predatory birds are found throughout much of the world, apart from various remote islands and Antarctica. In many species, the plumage of males and females is identical, but hens can generally be identified by their larger size. The majority of owls nest in cavities in trees, although some prefer cliff ledges, while the barn owl breeds within the confines of a building.

Owls have even managed to colonize areas where there are no trees at all, for example, in the tundra region of the Northern Hemisphere. Here, the aptly named snowy owl nests on the ground, choosing a raised spot that will give it a view of potential predators. The almost pure white plumage of the males enables them to blend in against the snowy background of this landscape, while females show a much more striking pattern of barring that helps to conceal them when they are nesting on the ground.

Unlike most other species, snowy owls must hunt in daylight, because for part of the year there is always light in the high latitudes where they live. They feed mainly on lemmings and arctic hares, and the availability of prey has a significant impact on their breeding success. This tends to be cyclical; in good years, parents may successfully rear seven youngsters, but when prey is scarce, only one or two offspring may survive to fledging.

In some areas, the use of chemicals throughout the food chain has also had an effect on the breeding capacity of owls. Poisons used to kill rodents can build up within the owl's body, causing weakness in the structure of the eggshell and a dramatic decline in hatchability. However, now that the harmful impact of these chemicals has become clear, there are moves to ban their use around the world.

Above: A young snowy owl in immature plumage. Nesting in the Arctic tundra, the numbers of chicks reared depend on the supply of food, notably lemmings, in this bleak terrain.

Right: A female snowy owl at her nest at Cambridge Bay in the Northwest Territory of Canada. The owlets' coloration helps to conceal their presence, but they often fall prey to foxes, in spite of their parents' care.

Left: The great horned owl ranges from the far north of Canada south across the whole of South America. The tufts of feathers on the head give rise to the common name. It is smaller than the European horned owl.

Left: Great horned owls usually produce just two or three chicks, but up to six when their prey (the hare) is abundant.

Left: The coloration of the screech owl varies and provides appropriate camouflage for the area concerned. The grey form shown here lives in conifer forests, unlike the rufous form.

Below: Young screech owls at their nest site in a tree. Most screech owls are found in areas of forest, where they hunt insects, such as moths, at night. Larger species prey on rodents.

Below: A young long-eared owl. This Northern Hemisphere species is nocturnal, but may hunt before dusk when there are chicks to be fed. Young leave the nest at about 25 days, but will not be able to fly for 10 days.

Right: The unusual name of the saw-whet owl comes from one of its calls, which resembles a saw being sharpened. It nests in tree holes. Young birds are white at first, then moult into chocolate brown juvenile plumage.

OSTRICHES – THE LARGEST LIVING BIRDS

Ostriches are found in many parts of Africa. They gather in groups of up to 50 birds, although there appears to be no real social structure in such flocks. Unable to fly, ostriches rely on their running skills and powerful legs – terminating in sharp claws – to escape the attentions of possible predators.

Breeding does leave them vulnerable, however, since they are forced to nest on the ground. Having selected a suitable spot, a female ostrich excavates a hollow scrape in the ground and lays up to 12 eggs. Other females may be attracted to the nest site, laying their eggs here as well, so that ultimately there may be 30 or more eggs in the nest.

As might be expected from the largest of all living birds, ostriches lay the largest eggs and these are accepted as the biggest single cell in the world. The eggs of ostriches in the north of Africa are heavier than those from other parts of their range, weighing up to 1.65kg(3lb 10oz). Each egg measures over 15cm(6in) long and 12.5cm(5in) wide. The shell is particularly robust, being 1.6mm(0.06in) thick and capable of withstanding the weight of an average person. The broken shells of ostrich eggs have been used as cups by various ancient civilizations.

The cock ostrich undertakes most of the incubation duties, although the hen may take over for part of the day, and the heat of the sun ensures that the eggs are warmed when the nest is left uncovered. The chicks hatch after about 40 days; at this stage, they are approximately 30cm(12in) tall. They are soon able to move at speed with their parents if danger threatens and, if necessary, can also pretend to be dead, which deters many active predators. This behaviour may also have given rise to the expression 'burying your head in the sand like an ostrich' – hoping a problem will simply go away by doing nothing.

Above: A family group of ostriches in southern Africa. Guarded by their parents, the chicks grow rapidly, reaching virtually their full height within 12 months. They may start to breed from about three or four years.

Below: Ostrich eggs are laid in a shallow scrape on the ground. Many of them are destroyed by hyenas and jackals before they have an opportunity to hatch.

Below: The young ostrich emerges in a relatively advanced state of development. Its coloration helps to provide camouflage in open country.

Above: Ostriches are mainly herbivorous in their feeding habits, but may consume insects and small animals as well.

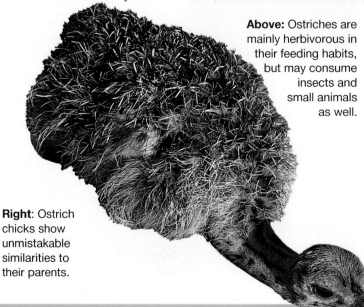

Right: Ostrich chicks show unmistakable similarities to their parents.

Left: The paired female remains with the cock and can apparently recognize her own eggs, discarding those of other hens. The circular shape of the egg makes it easier to roll from the nest. Both parents share the task of incubation, with the hen sitting during the day and the male taking over at dusk.

Below: The ostrich's keen eyesight gives an early indication of danger. It relies on speed to outrun predators and can attain 50kph(31mph) for a considerable distance. The powerful legs terminate in two toes. If cornered, ostriches can kick with considerable force, and have been known to kill people.

Below: More than one hen will lay her eggs in an ostrich nest. Before incubation begins in earnest, the number of eggs will be reduced to about 20, the maximum that an ostrich can incubate properly. In spite of their tough shells, the eggs may be cracked by Egyptian vultures, found across much of Africa. They break the eggs by dropping stones on them.

Below: An ostrich egg. Note its unusual circular shape. Incubation lasts about 40 days, and young ostriches have a very long life expectancy. They may well live for over 60 years.

PENGUINS – SURVIVING AGAINST THE ODDS

Penguins occur in some of the coldest areas of the Southern Hemisphere, including the Antarctic, and face particular problems when breeding. However, studies have shown that successive generations of these birds have returned to the same sites to breed for about 700 years. Some penguins nest in huge colonies, consisting of half a million individuals.

The breeding habits of the emperor penguin, one of the Antarctic species, are unusual in many respects. Firstly, they start to nest in the autumn, rather than in spring, emerging from the freezing water to journey to their breeding grounds. After a brief courtship, the female penguin lays her single egg, which is transferred almost immediately to the male's care. She then travels back to the sea and feeds for the first time in perhaps two months.

The males huddle together in groups called pods, in temperatures that fall far below freezing point. The egg rests on top of their feet and is tucked in tightly

amongst the feathers. Even a momentary exposure to the air would be fatal for the embryo in this harsh environment. Just over two months after it was laid, the young penguin hatches and is fed by the male. At this stage, the adult females return to the group, relieving their mates, whose body weight will probably have fallen by about one third during this period.

Now it is the turn of the male penguins to return to the sea to feed, before they, too, finally return to help the females rear the chicks. As the young penguins become independent, at about four months old, it is summer again in the Southern Hemisphere and conditions are at their most favourable to ensure the survival of the youngsters at this early stage.

Left: An adelie penguin chick with its mother. This species is characterized by the white area of skin encircling each eye. All 18 penguin species live only in the Southern Hemisphere.

Above: Two young chinstrap penguins beg for food. Breeding occurs in the short Antarctic summer, when conditions are less intimidating than during the rest of the year. Chinstraps breed in vast colonies of up to two million individuals. It takes about five weeks for the eggs to hatch. Before taking to water, the young congregate in groups of up to 200 individuals, called kindergartens. They will begin to swim from about nine weeks old.

Above: The emperor penguin is the largest of all species and lives mainly within the Antarctic circle. These young chicks are duller in coloration than adults.

Left: A king penguin rookery on the island of South Georgia. The birds were hunted during the nineteenth century and became extinct in some areas.

Below: A pair of gentoo penguins display at the nest site. Three distinct races have been identified, with some populations breeding where there is no growing vegetation. However, as this photo shows, gentoos also nest in milder areas, building nests close to the shore in tussocks of grass. Their calls are like those of a braying donkey.

Left: A Gentoo penguin and chicks. It hunts almost exclusively for crabs. Like other species, it is well protected against the cold by a dense covering of body fat. Individual birds weigh about 5.5kg(12lb).

SEALS – BORN INTO A WORLD OF ICE

Seals are found along the shores of both the Arctic and Antarctic ice caps, as well as close to numerous rocky islands and similar localities where they will be reasonably safe from predators. These marine mammals spend most of their lives at sea, coming on land to give birth. It is advantageous if mating coincides with the period when the widest selection of mates is available. At breeding time, male seals often battle to establish their own harems, jealously guarding them from potential rivals, whereas at other times of the year they tend to lead solitary lives.

Seals mate in the normal mammalian way but, instead of developing immediately, the fertilized egg remains in the mother's tract for up to three and a half months. After this period of 'suspended animation', the egg implants normally into the wall of the uterus, the placenta forms to nourish the young seal and pregnancy begins in earnest. It lasts on average between 10 and 11 months, including the stage of so-called 'delayed implantation'. The advantage of delayed implantation is that the young can be born at a time most suited to their survival – vital in an area where food may be in short supply.

The young seals may be born on the open ice or, in some cases, in special lairs constructed by the female. She tunnels through the ice, excavating a chamber rather like an igloo beneath the snow. Here, the young seals are less likely to be seen by potential predators, such as polar bears. The snug lair also helps to keep the young pup warm, at a stage when it lacks the thick insulating layer of blubber beneath its skin that develops in older seals.

Above: A northern fur seal pup. Although widely distributed, this species has suffered greatly at the hands of sealers, with the population on the Pribilof Islands, close to the coast of North America, declining from about 4.5 million individuals in 1870 to just 200,000 in 1914.

Below: Weddell seals in Antarctica. Here they hunt fish beneath the ice, coming up to breathe in air holes, which they may enlarge and keep open with their teeth. Females give birth on the ice, and the babies have thick grey coats. They may be hunted by killer whales.

Left: The baby hooded seal has a slightly furry appearance, because its coat does not lie flat and the silvery blue coloration of the young pups has led to them being known as 'bluebacks'. Most births take place in late March and early April. The pups, weighing about 20kg(44lb) suckle for about two weeks and then the females mate again and head back to sea. The youngsters, sustained by fat, soon head off into water.

Left: A four-week-old Weddell seal pup suckles from its mother. The pups, born in September and October have greyish coats, but start to moult to resemble adults at about this age.

Below: A harbour seal and pup, which sheds its whitish coat soon after birth. This species seems to prefer relatively shallow coastal waters, and may venture into freshwater areas.

Right: A newly born harp seal. The seals tend to congregate at specific spots on the ice and return annually to give birth. The demand for their pelts has resulted in millions being killed.

Left: Young elephant seals battle playfully with each other. These are the largest seals, with big bulls weighing as much as 3,700kg(8,160lb). Their common name comes from the elongated nose of adult males, which is suggestive of an elephant's trunk. It can hang down over the mouth but, during the breeding period, it becomes more erect, helping to carry the bull's warning bellow over long distances. Bulls fight each other at this time for dominance and mating follows birth of the pups.

LION CUBS – LEARNING BY EXAMPLE

The lion is more social by nature than other big cats and lives in family groups called prides. Each pride consists of females with their cubs and probably at least one male. The size of the pride varies, depending on where the lions live; where the countryside has little cover, the number of lions in the pride tends to be larger. This probably helps them when they hunt, with the members of the pride working together and thus increasing the chances of making a kill.

Breeding can take place at any stage during the year, but it is usual for lionesses within a particular pride to give birth in the same period. Dominant males may move from one pride to another, fathering offspring in each case. Pregnancy lasts for about 15 weeks and a typical litter consists of three or four cubs – although, occasionally, as many as six may be born.

Each cub weighs about 1.3kg (almost 3lb) at birth, and it can take up to two weeks for their eyes to open completely. Cubs may suckle from a number of females in the pride, and so the burden of rearing them can be shared. Weaning is unlikely to take place for at least six months, and the young lions will start to hunt with the pride when they are about eleven months old. At this stage, they have much to learn from their elders – if the youngsters reveal their presence too soon, for example, then the prey will be lost. The young lions will probably be unable to make a kill on their own until they are nearly 16 months old.

By this stage, the female will begin to accept the attentions of males again. Most lionesses will start to breed by the time they are four years old, and then have a litter every second year. Young males may be driven out of the pride, however, and forced to live on their own until they establish their own territories.

Above: Lion cubs are born into a group called a pride. Its female members are likely to be related, and there may well be a strong bond between them. Young lionesses often stay as part of the pride for their entire lives.

Below: Playing together in the Masai Mara National Park in Kenya, these cubs are learning essential survival skills. Little tolerance is shown towards the cubs at a kill and they may have to battle for a share of food.

Left: A lion cub is as appealing as a baby kitten, but it could weigh up to 250kg (55lb) when adult, and eat 40kg(88lb) of food at a time. Its survival depends on the hunting skills of its pride.

Right: These lion cubs are about three weeks old and will stay with their mother for three months. They also suckle from other lionesses in the pride.

Above: Four cubs form a typical litter. Within a pride, groups of cubs play together, but rest at the hottest time of the day.

Left: Lionesses move their cubs around in their mouths, carrying them by the scruff of the neck, without hurting them.

Below: This two-week-old cub is gnawing playfully on its mother's leg. Soon, its first milk teeth will appear. These develop within the first month of life and enable the cub to take morsels of meat. The permanent teeth erupt from nine months onwards – often a painful experience.

Above: These cubs, born just two weeks previously, suckle from their mother. Lionesses are normally very tolerant, and do not resent other cubs suckling from them as well.

Left: Licking the cub after suckling can encourage it to defaecate. Other females in the pride may groom the cubs in a similar fashion, and this will be permitted by their mother. Most lionesses prove good mothers.

TIGERS – BORN TO LIVE ALONE

The range of these majestic cats has shrunk noticeably during the twentieth century, but they are still present throughout a wide area of Southeast Asia. For most of the year, tigers live solitary lives and it is only during the mating period that males and females are seen together. At this stage, males become very territorial and will fight to the death with a potential rival. The breeding period varies according to the area concerned. In Manchuria (a region of northeastern China), breeding takes place during December, while further south, it can occur at virtually any time of year.

Tigers are generally mature by the time they are three or four years old. During the few days when the female is receptive, mating may take place over 100 times. Subsequently, both partners go their separate ways, and after a gestation period of about 15 weeks, the female gives birth to her litter in a den. On average, three or four cubs are born, each one weighing about 1kg(2.2lb) and already showing the characteristic stripes on their coats. They are blind and totally dependent on their mother at this stage, but they develop very rapidly. After two weeks, they are able to see, and by the time they are two months old they start to venture out with their mother. However, they will not be weaned until they are 18 months old. Although they may occasionally catch prey, it seems that during this period they are learning the necessary hunting skills from their mother. They may remain within her territory even after they are independent, but the youngsters finally leave to establish their own territories by the time they are 30 months old.

Above: Born in a sheltered cave or thick vegetation, tiger cubs are helpless at birth. In spite of their mother's care, about half the cubs in each litter will not survive to independence. Their maximum lifespan is likely to be about 26 years. Adult females will not give birth again until their previous cubs have left, so litters are produced every two years.

Left: A Siberian tiger cub. These are the biggest of all living cats. In winter their coat becomes paler, enabling them to conceal themselves in the snow. They occur in southeast Siberia and Manchuria, their last remaining stronghold being the Ussuri region of the Soviet Union.

Left: A baby Sumatran tiger. Only about 1,000 individuals of this race, confined to the island of Sumatra, off the coast of Southeast Asia, still survive. Hunting and deforestation pose a serious threat to tigers in many parts of their wide range. If numbers fall too low, breeding is unlikely to be successful and localized populations die out, as in the case of the Bali tiger, once found on the nearby Indonesian island. It became extinct in 1937.

Right: Tigers are highly secretive, but are found in a wide variety of terrains, as long as there is sufficient cover for them to hunt effectively. Unlike many cats, tigers do not avoid water and can swim up to 29km(18miles). Young tigers occasionally climb trees, but older individuals rarely do. They learn hunting skills from their mother. This family will need about 280kg(618lb) of meat every three weeks to sustain them.

Above: Tigers are often found in the vicinity of water holes. Here, likely prey will come to drink and, if there is adequate cover, the tiger will be able to make a kill. Having eaten its fill, the tiger conceals the remains of the animal under vegetation, and returns later on to feed again.

Right: A baby Siberian tiger bred in captivity. Co-ordinated breeding programmes offer hope of saving the endangered races from extinction. The reputation of the tiger as a killer of people is exaggerated. Usually, only old or sick animals will attack; they have difficulty hunting other prey.

COYOTES – WILD DOGS THAT LOOK AFTER THEIR OWN

As wolves have declined in number throughout North America during recent years, so their adaptable relative, the coyote has increased its range. These wild dogs, sometimes called prairie wolves, are now found from Costa Rica northwards to Alaska. Coyotes were first reported from New York State in 1925, crossing into Massachusetts by 1957 and then reaching the shores of Hudson Bay four years later.

They are primarily scavengers, hunting on their own or with a partner, and not now believed to be a danger to cattle, although many thousands of coyotes have been killed in the past as a serious threat to farmstock. Examination of their stomach contents has shown that they prey mainly on rabbits and, sometimes, chickens.

The pair bond between coyotes is strong and may last for life, having been forged by the time they are about a year old. Mating takes place during the early months of the year, and the pair seek a suitable den where their pups can be born. They may take over an existing hole, such as a fox earth, and enlarge it to form an underground tunnel. This can be 9m(30ft) long, and up to 60cm(2ft) wide, terminating in the nesting chamber. On occasion, coyotes may even choose a suitable hole in a tree above ground. Pregnancy lasts about 63 days, with between five and seven pups normally being born, although double this number is not unknown. At this stage, the male coyote moves to another den nearby, but returns regularly with food for the family. It is not unknown for two females to share a den, and if only one has pups, the other assists the male in providing food for the litter.

Above: A coyote pup resembles a domestic dog. Cross-breeding can occur and the resulting pups are known as coydogs.

Left: Young coyotes first leave the den at five or six weeks old. If they venture too far, they track back by means of scent.

Below: Coyote pups will start to hunt from two months old, and the family group breaks up towards the end of summer. The young wander off on their own and, if they manage to survive, finally establish a territory.

Above: Many dangers lie ahead of young coyotes. Some simply die of starvation, others from human persecution, or they may fall victim to wolves and jaguars. Coyotes are not well equipped to hunt in snow, and winter can be a difficult time for them. They may resort to fishing in rivers or through holes in the ice.

Right: A young coyote pup on its own may keep in contact with other coyotes by barking. Their calls carry over a wide area.

Below: It is not unknown for coyotes to eat plants and other vegetation. As well as grass, they consume nuts and even parts of the prickly pear cactus.

Below: As coyotes move into urban areas, there is a greater risk of coydogs being produced. These can breed twice a year. However, wolves kill coyotes and do not mate with them.

ELEPHANTS – BORN INTO A MATRIARCHY

In elephant communities, the cow is the dominant herd member. Bulls tend to associate in loose groups or lead solitary lives but, during the breeding period, they may compete with one another to mate with a female. The breeding habits of both the African and Asian elephant are similar. Within the elephants' range, breeding activity is linked to the onset of the rainy season, which triggers the growth of vegetation and, therefore, increases the protein level in the diet.

Elephants are likely to be mature by the time they are 14 years old. The reproductive anatomy of bull elephants is unusual, because the testes are retained within the body, rather than descending into a scrotal sac as is usually the case in mammals. After mating, pregnancy lasts between 17 and 25 months, with 22 months being the average. In most cases, a single youngster is born, but in about one birth per hundred, twins will result. Young elephants are quite mobile and able to stand within half an hour of birth. However, the herd will pause at this stage and wait for a day or so, until the youngster is strong enough to walk with them. Measuring about 91cm(36in) at the shoulder, a newborn elephant weighs up to 120kg

(264lb). It uses its mouth to suckle from its mother's paired mammary glands, located between the front legs. Weaning takes place within three years.

Adult females give birth to about five offspring during their reproductive lives. Older cows still have an important role to play within the herd as matriarchal figures, guiding younger individuals around the territory. This learning process plays a vital part in ensuring the continued well-being of the herd, especially when food and water are in short supply.

Below: A baby elephant bathing at a water hole in the Etosha National Park, Namibia in southwestern Africa. Bathing is important for elephants as it helps to cool their large bodies.

Right: Young African elephants are born without tusks. These only start to become apparent from the age of about two years onwards. Tusks are modified forms of the upper incisor teeth.

Left: Young elephants are protected by other members of the herd. Adults face few dangers, apart from poachers, but youngsters are vulnerable to large predators if left alone. Twin births are rare but not unknown, occurring about once in every hundred pregnancies.

Right: The elephant's trunk is an essential tool, acting rather like a hand. The tip contains the nostrils, and also present here are flattened areas top and bottom, which resemble fingers. Elephants use their trunks for a variety of tasks, such as lifting objects and eating. As well as sucking up water and squirting it into the mouth, this youngster may also spray itself.

Left: Older members of a herd will break off branches for youngsters. Baby elephants are born with a thin covering of brown hair, but this soon disappears as they grow older.

Below: Elephant calves may wander off on their own, and so it is not unusual for one herd member to supervise the youngsters, especially at a water hole, where they enjoy bathing and playing for long periods.

ZEBRAS – READY TO RUN WITHIN THE HOUR

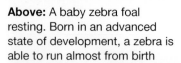

These members of the horse family tend to be found in family groups, with one stallion living in the company of several mares and their offspring. The males that oversee a group of females tend to be the strongest, fittest individuals. Younger and older zebras gather in separate stallion herds, with the former moving into the territories of established stallions and displacing them as they mature. Initially, a male challenges a rival by a pushing contest, but this can develop into a more serious encounter, backed by biting and kicking.

Following mating, pregnancy lasts just over a year. As with other horses, only a single offspring results; twins, when they do occur, do not prove viable. A young zebra measures about 84cm(33in) at the shoulder, and weighs up to 35kg(77lb) at birth. It will be up on its feet and capable of running within an hour, which minimizes the risk of predation by lions and other hunters that often prey on zebras.

Although young zebras can be observed grazing when only one month old, the weaning process is much more protracted, taking place over 8-13 months. It is quite possible for a female to mate again almost immediately after giving birth, but the rate of conception at this stage is quite low. On average, female zebras breed once every three years.

Females leave the group when they are two years old, often taken by a passing male in the area. Young males ultimately join up with a bachelor herd, before forcing their way into an existing group at about five years old to establish their own group of females. In normal circumstances, zebras may live over 20 years, at least in captivity, where life is less hazardous.

Above: A baby zebra foal resting. Born in an advanced state of development, a zebra is able to run almost from birth should danger threaten. Its stripes are brown rather than black, and the mane is likely to be shorter than in adults.

Left: In spite of their docile appearance, zebras can be very aggressive in defence of their foals. Attacking lions are known to have been badly injured by a group of determined zebras.

Above: A Grevy's zebra with her foal. Their stripes are closely spaced and extend right down the legs, as far as the hooves. The stripe pattern distinguishes the three species of zebra.

Left: Three distinct species of zebra live in Africa. They can be distinguished not only by their markings, but also by their habits. Grevy's zebra from the northeastern part of their range is the least social. In these zebras, no permanent bond is formed between adults, who wander alone or in small groups. Stallions are much more tolerant of each other than in the other species. Male Grevy's zebras have the largest territories of all herbivores; these may extend over 10.5sq.km(4sq.miles). Large piles of dung are often used to mark the territorial boundaries.

Left: An orphaned zebra foal. Deprived of its mother's milk, its chances of survival are poor. It may succumb to disease or fall victim to a predator. Speed and its powerful hind legs are its best defence.

Below: A four-month-old Buchell's foal with its mother on the Serengeti plains of Tanzania, East Africa. Studies have shown that zebras can communicate by means of a variety of postural movements. They can also vocalize, and may bray to each other over longer distances.

WILD BOARS – STRIPED FOR CAMOUFLAGE AT BIRTH

These ancestors of today's pigs still live in the wild, in groups called sounders made up of females (sows) and their offspring. The males (boars), by contrast, tend to live mainly on their own. They all forage for a variety of foods, ranging from acorns and fruit to roots, which they dig up.

In a given area, there will be an order of dominance among the boars. The courtship process begins when a boar pushes gently at the sow's flanks and tries to rest his head on her rump. If the sow is ready to mate, this action will prompt her to position herself for the purpose. Although boars may be mature by the time they are 18 months old, it tends to be the older individuals, approaching four years of age, that mate.

There are nine species of wild pig, and those that live within the tropics may breed at any time of the year. However, the wild boar found in Europe and other more temperate climates tends to mate in the autumn. The resulting piglets are born in the spring after a gestation period of about 14 weeks. Litter size is quite variable, ranging from two up to twelve. Before giving birth, the sow makes a grass nest for her offspring and there they will stay for a week or so. From then on, they start to follow their mother around, although they will not be weaned until they are about three months old.

The young piglets are striped at first, and these markings may act as cryptic camouflage, helping to conceal their presence in the open areas of woodland where they live. Even after they are weaned, the piglets tend to stay close to their mother in the existing herd, until she is ready to give birth again during the following year.

Above: A European wild boar with her piglets. Today, the range of this species is greatly reduced, because of hunting pressures and the increasing urbanization in Europe.

Right: Young wild boar are likely to stay with their mother for up to two years. This means that the previous year's offspring may live alongside the piglets.

Right: In tropical areas, as here on the Indonesian island of Bali, breeding can take place at any time of year; in Europe, piglets are normally born in the spring.

Below: Domestication of the pig probably began in China, about 7,000 years ago. Spanish settlers first brought wild boar to the southeastern United States during the sixteenth century and now it is established there.

Above: A group of Vietnamese pot-bellied piglets. Young pigs snuggle up together like this to conserve their body heat. Pigs are opportunist feeders and will feed on human garbage, so it is not surprising that they were kept as a source of meat from an early stage in history.

Below: Domestic pigs differ from their wild ancestors by generally having a lighter and less dense covering of bristles. However, they have maintained many of their behavioural characteristics, such as mud-bathing. This cools the skin and protects against parasites.

Left: The sensitive snout of the wild boar helps the animal find food. It is protected by a small bone. As a result, pigs use the snout as well as the forefeet for digging up roots, tubers and other edible items.

Right: At first, there may be some dispute about which piglet feeds from which nipple, but soon a dominance hierarchy is established within the litter. Piglets suckle for three months, but will also have begun to take solid food during this period.

FAWNS – BEAUTIFUL AND APPEALING BABY DEER

The 38 recognized species of deer have a wide distribution across all continents, apart from the southern part of Africa. Their characteristic horns, known as antlers, are present on males of all types of deer and on female reindeer. These outgrowths from the skull have a bony centre, and are used both to deter predators and as 'status symbols' to establish an order of dominance within the herd.

In North America and Europe, deer start to grow their antlers in early summer, and as autumn approaches they reach their maximum size. The antlers are first covered in a thin layer of skin called velvet, which becomes torn to reveal the bone beneath as the deer rub their antlers against branches and other places. Mating takes place at this time, with stags frequently challenging each other over access to the females. Pregnancy lasts about 5-10 months, depending on species. In roe deer, the fertilized egg does not develop immediately, but may remain in a state of suspended animation for four months or so before it implants into the female's uterus. This ensures that whenever mating occurs the young will be born in the spring, increasing the likelihood of their survival. Deer living in tropical areas may breed at any stage throughout the year, and so do not shed their antlers in late winter as do species in temperate areas.

Generally, female deer, known as hinds, give birth to only one or two fawns – although, occasionally, up to four may be produced. A baby fawn is one of the

most appealing sights in nature, and has become celebrated in the cinema through Walt Disney's cartoon film 'Bambi'. Young deer develop their antlers slowly – during their first year or two, they appear just as spikes. Only as the deer approach maturity will the antlers assume the shape characteristic of their species.

Left: A white-bellied deer hind with her fawn. Youngsters suckle about once every four hours.

Below: A group of red deer hinds with their fawns in the spring. Stags tend to live apart until the start of the mating season during the autumn.

Above: A newborn black-tail deer fawn remains motionless, so as not to alert predators to its presence. These deer normally produce twin offspring.

Below: A sika deer fawn. These hardy Asiatic deer are born in summer after a 39-week pregnancy, and may live 25 years.

Above: White-tailed deer are soon independent, being suckled for just one month in some cases. They rest hidden in vegetation, and will be fed by their mother every four hours.

Below: A white-tailed hind with two fawns. These New World deer generally prefer an area with adequate vegetation to conceal them. They are most active at dawn and dusk.

Left: Female roe deer establish territories, both when mating and giving birth, which they defend. Licking the fawn helps to keep it odourless, so it is less easily detected by potential predators.

Below: A day-old white-tailed deer fawn. Born in a relatively advanced state of development, it is able to stand almost immediately after birth, and will soon be nibbling at vegetation.

WILD SHEEP – HARDY HERBIVORES

Wild sheep and goats are closely related herbivores, belonging to a group known as the goat antelopes. Although there is some disagreement over their classification, it is generally accepted that eight species of sheep can be identified. They tend to be found in temperate areas of the world, often at relatively high altitudes. During the summer, they range over a wide area, moving into the valleys at the start of winter to seek protection from the worst of the weather.

Wild sheep are often seen in herds made up of both sexes, although in some cases the males (rams) live separately. Mating tends to take place throughout the autumn, extending into winter. Following a gestation period of 21-26 weeks, the young lambs are born in the spring, which ensures that they will have the benefit of a summer's grazing before facing up to the relative harshness of winter.

The number of offspring depends on the species concerned. While some may produce only a single lamb, others – including the domestic sheep – can produce up to four offspring at a time. Weighing on average 3-5kg(7-12lb), the young lambs are born in a relatively advanced state of development and can run around almost from birth. As they grow older, they tend to split off, forming their own groups, and only return to suckle from their mothers.

In most cases, young females (ewes) will not mate before their second year, whereas rams may have to wait until they are seven years old. This is because the ram with the biggest horns is the dominant member of the group and, although persistently challenged, he is unlikely to be displaced by much younger individuals. In time, however, young rams can make an effective challenge and achieve mating rights. The majority of wild sheep live for ten years on average, although it is possible for them to survive into their twenties if conditions are favourable.

Left: A Rocky Mountain bighorn lamb, about three weeks old. Most wild sheep are found in upland areas; this species ranges from Canada through the western part of the United States to Mexico. They are both agile climbers and strong swimmers.

Left: North American mountain goat kid. Sheep and goats are herbivorous, and will also travel in search of essential minerals.

Right: A goat with her kid. The distinction between sheep and goats is not entirely clear-cut but, as a general rule, the horns of goats grow vertically and curve backwards, whereas a sheep's horns are directed over the sides of its head. The shape of the goat's forehead is convex, rather than concave as in sheep. Male goats (billies) have a beard and generally have a strong odour associated with them.

Above: Skipping and jumping from rock to rock, lambs reveal their upland ancestry. These skills are essential for survival.

Right: A lamb suckles from a ewe. As it grows, the lamb must kneel down on its forelegs to reach the mammary glands.

Left: Mountain goats mate in the winter, with the kids being born in early summer. Although single births are most common, twins or even triplets are not unknown. The young are able to follow their mothers within a week and are driven off in the autumn, just before mating takes place again.

Right: Dall sheep in Alaska. Dominant rams have large curved horns used in ritual battles for supremacy, but rarely to inflict serious injuries. Young males battle against established rams, but are handicapped by their smaller horns.

RABBITS AND HARES – ADAPTABLE AND FERTILE

Rabbits and hares – collectively known as lagomorphs – are found on all continents of the world, apart from Antarctica, and in a wide range of environments. Whereas some of the 44 species have adapted to live in tropical forests, others thrive in semi-desert conditions, and the arctic hare, as its name suggests, inhabits the far north, where there is often snow on the ground.

The major factors underlying the success of lagomorphs are their adaptability and high reproductive rate. When conditions are favourable, rabbits and hares can spread rapidly, sometimes with devastating effects on agriculture, since these herbivores feed mainly on vegetation.

Rabbits give birth either within a warren – a series of tunnels and chambers where they live when not foraging above ground – or they may use a special breeding 'stop', a shallow tunnel dug in the ground to shelter the litter. Pregnancy lasts about four weeks, and just before giving birth to as many as eight offspring, the female rabbit plucks her fur to make a soft lining for the nest. Baby rabbits, known as kittens, are born blind and naked.

Surprisingly, it is now clear that rabbits only suckle their youngsters very briefly, for perhaps five minutes every day. Weaning takes place about three weeks after birth and the young rabbits become mature by the time they are three months old. However, they face a life full of hazards, including over 40 species of predators in Europe alone. Most rabbits survive for less than a year in the wild.

Young hares, called leverets, are born in a more advanced state of development, with their eyes open and a covering of fur. They tend to mature later than rabbits, rarely breeding until they are over a year old and, on rare occasions, may survive for 10 or more years in the wild.

Left: Cottontails are solitary rabbits, with does establishing their own territories. A buck will defend its area using its strong hind feet.

Above: A baby cottontail rabbit. These rabbits are born in simple nests on the ground. Over three-quarters of young cottontails die before they are 12 months, but a few may live up to 10 years.

Above: A snowshoe hare from North America, showing the characteristic white winter coat that helps to conceal it in a snowy landscape. The large hind feet are covered in especially thick hair, enabling the hare to walk through deep snow without becoming trapped. In winter it often hides close to trees, but in summer it favours a den in thick forest.

Right: Baby snowshoe hares are born between April and June. Females may have three litters in succession, producing up to 13 offspring in one year.

Below: Huddled together in a snug nest, baby rabbits sit quietly. This is one of their best defences against predators, from eagles launching aerial attacks to foxes and dogs.

Left: These fluffy angora babies are just one of over 100 breeds of domestic rabbit. They are especially prized for the fine quality of their wool, which is used to make various garments.

Right: Females that mate again days before giving birth, can carry both the young about to be born and the newly fertilized eggs at the same time.

KANGAROOS – SUCCESSFUL POUCHED MAMMALS

Kangaroos are found only in Australia and New Guinea. They belong to a group of mammals known as marsupials that have a pouch in which the young develop outside the reproductive tract. The gestation period of the kangaroo embryo is remarkably short, often lasting only four or five weeks from mating. The red kangaroo, the largest of the marsupials, reaches 90kg(198lb) when adult, but starts its life as a tiny creature weighing just 0.75gm(0.026oz).

The newly born kangaroo climbs unerringly up and into its mother's pouch, anchoring onto a nipple. Here it remains for about 70 days, only starting to look out of the pouch when it is over 20 weeks old. Twins are occasionally recorded, but it is unlikely that both will survive in the pouch. The youngster – known as a joey – will start to leave its mother's pouch from 27 weeks old, scurrying back if it is frightened. After a further six weeks, it will have outgrown the pouch, but still suckles here by placing its head inside at intervals.

Some kangaroos breed throughout the year, whereas other species have a more clearly defined breeding period, often linked to the onset of the rainy season. It is not unusual for females to have an embryo in the reproductive tract, a joey in the pouch and a third, older youngster still accompanying her. Should a single joey die in the pouch at an early stage, the fertilized egg in the reproductive tract will begin its development. After giving birth, the female will mate again, ensuring as far as possible that she is always fertile should she lose her current offspring. This unusual method of reproduction has clearly proved successful in biological terms, since kangaroos are abundant in many parts of their range.

Above: A young grey kangaroo grooms itself outside the pouch. Kangaroo numbers in Australia have grown as a result of agricultural development, which has led to water being more readily available in dry areas. Kangaroos graze on the shorter pasture, while farmstock eats the longer, coarser grass.

Below: A joey peeps out of its mother's pouch. Originally it was believed that the joey was born in the pouch, but in fact it instinctively crawls there at an early stage of development. Not until 1923 did zoologists finally accept this explanation of the phenomenon, following observations of captive animals.

Left: A mother and her 'joey' engage in a friendly tussle. But kangaroos have sharp claws on their forelimbs and can inflict painful injuries if threatened. At one time, dingos kept kangaroo numbers in check, but they have been virtually exterminated in many areas. Now kangaroos face virtually no predators, but they are hunted, and a number are killed on the roads at night. Young joeys in the pouch may survive such accidents and there are sanctuaries in Australia that will rear these orphans.

Above: Larger kangaroos, such as the antilopine, live in groups. Some breed all year; others for a limited period.

Left: As joeys grow older, they spend longer out of the pouch. When they do return, they may lie at a peculiar angle, with one or more legs protruding.

Below: Even when it is too big to fit into the pouch, the young kangaroo continues suckling. This whiptail wallaby is fast approaching independence.

Above: Young kangaroos are unlikely to breed for the first time until they are at least 20 months. They may live for over 20 years.

Left: The red kangaroo is the largest marsupial and despite its size, its young develop faster than some smaller kangaroos. Usually found in mobs of up to a dozen, it occurs across virtually all of Australia. If adequate food and water are available, red kangaroos will breed all year. Females mate again two days after giving birth.

ORANG-UTANS – OUR CLOSEST RELATIVES

Confined to the islands of Borneo and Sumatra, off the coast of Southeast Asia, the orang-utans are one of our closest relatives in the animal world. Their faces, like our own, are very distinctive and they may change as the animals grow older.

Orang-utans are forest-dwellers, swinging through the branches using their long arms. But they can also walk on the ground, although in the wild this is unusual; generally, only the heavier, older males are encountered on the floor of the forest. Each evening, orang-utans build a nest to sleep in. This takes the form of a simple platform of leaves and twigs, covered with a roof to protect themselves from the rain.

Baby orang-utans can be born at any stage during the year, with pregnancy lasting nine months. At birth, the youngster will weigh about 1.8kg(4lb), and has a thin covering of hair on its back and head. The baby stays close to its mother, gripping the hair of her underparts as she moves through the trees. It will be three years before the young orang-utan is weaned, and after this, the youngster will probably remain with its mother for a further two or three years. As adolescence approaches, orang-utans form small groups on their own, feeding and playing together, but adults live fairly solitary lives when not breeding.

Female orang-utans may start breeding by the time they are 10 years old, but it is likely to be several more years before males establish their own territories and start to mate. Orang-utans can live for over 30 years, but hunting and forest clearance represent serious threats to their survival throughout their range.

Above: Maternal care is a common feature in the higher apes, which are man's closest living relatives. The close bond established between mother and baby will last for years, even after the weaning stage has passed. Like man, orang-utans mature slowly, and normally have a long reproductive life.

Left: Orphaned orang-utans, whose mothers have been killed, are being hand-reared in a special sanctuary at Bohorok in Sumatra. It is hoped to release them in due course. Orang-utans are well adapted for life in the treetops. They use their long arms to swing through the forest, leaping from branch to branch.

Right: This tender picture of a mother and baby emphasises how similar we are to the great apes. In the area where it occurs, the orang-utan is known to the native people as the 'old man of the forest'. Like children, young orang-utans must be taught how to survive on their own; this process may take five years.

Right: A 29-year old Bornean orang-utan with her six-week old youngster. Orang-utans only breed once every four years and this, coupled with their low birth rate, could threaten their existence.

Right: During her lifetime, a female orang-utan is unlikely to have more than four or five youngsters. In spite of the great care lavished upon them, the infant mortality rate is as high as 40 percent, so the population increases very slowly.

Below: Once ready to leave their mothers, young orang-utans join together to form their own groups. A mastery of climbing skills is essential for their survival. In dense forest they can communicate by 'burping' noises.

INDEX

Page numbers in **bold** indicate major references including accompanying photographs. Page numbers in *italics* indicate captions to other illustrations. Less important text entries are shown in normal type.

PICTURE CREDITS

Photographers
The publishers wish to thank the following photographers and agencies who have supplied photographs for this book. The photographers have been credited by page number and position on the page: (B) Bottom, (T) Top, (C) Centre, (BL) Bottom Left, etc.

Biofotos: 10(T, Heather Angel), 11(BL, Heather Angel, BR, Brian Rogers)

Marc Henrie: 54(BR)

Chris Mattison: 14(T,B), 15(B)

William A. Tomey: 8(B), 9, 11(T,C)

Photo Researchers Inc.:

James L. Amos: 22(BL)
Toni Angermayer: 40(T)
Robert J. Ashworth: 12(T)
Ron Austing: 25(BR), 31(TR)
Tom Bledsoe: 17(CR,BL), 36(T)
Malcolm Boulton: 46(T)
Mark N. Boulton: 39(CL), 47(T)
Ken Brate: 13(TR)
Julie Bruton: 44(BL)
Scott Camazine: 26(T,BR)
Alan D. Carey: 43(TL,BR), 53(BR)
William Curtsinger: 34(BR), 36(CR)
Ray Coleman: 6(T), 7(TR)
Stephen Dalton: 25(BL)
Treat Davidson: 16(CR)
Tim Davis: 33(TC), 38(T), 44(BR), 45(BR)
Gregory G. Dimijian: 7(CL), 10(CL), 35(TR), 37(B), 38(BR), 39(B), 47(BR)
Stephanie Dinkins: 17(BR)
R. D. Estes: 32(CR,BR), 47(BL)
Jack Fields: 48(B)
Kenneth W. Fink 20(BL)
Lowell Georgia: Copyright page (T)
Michael Giannechini: 30(BR)
Francois Gohier: 21(BL), 37(CT)
Jim W. Grace: 57(TR)
Jose Luis G. Grande: 13(BL), 24(B), 49(BL), 55(BR)
Gilbert S. Grant: 23(T)
Eunice Harris: 49(TL)
Phillip Hayson: 29(BL)
Robert Hermes: 16(BL)
Robert W. Hernandez: 22(T), 34(BL), 35(BR)
G. R. Higbee: 52(BL)
George Holton: Copyright page (B), 35(TL)
Mike James: 57(CL)
M. Philip Kahl: 45(BL)
G. C. Kelley: 21(CR), 54(BL)
Karl W. Kenyon: 23(BR)
Ted Kerasote: 38(CR)
Stephen J. Krasemann: 29(C), 39(T), 46(B), 55(CR)
Frans Lanting: 13(TL,CR,BR), 22(BR), 23(C,BL)

Robert Lee: 21(BR)
Pat & Tom Leeson: 7(CR), 41(BR), 43(TR), 50(T), 52(CR), 53(CL)
Jeff L. Lepore: 7(TL), 17(T,CL)
Norman R. Lightfoot: 25(TR), 30(T), 36(BL), 37(CB)
Christina Loke: 25(TL)
S. R. Maglione: 16(T)
Ferenc Magyar/Okapia: 51(CL)
Frank W. Mantlik: 19(B), 53(TL)
Karl & Steve Maslowski: 30(CR)
Steve Maslowski: 18(T), 20(CR)
Brock May: 19(TR)
Anthony Mercieca: 21(TL,TR)
Lawrence Migdale: 12(BL)
D. Mohrhardt: 28-9(T)
Ann Morgan: 32(T)
William H. Mullins: 31(BL), 53(TR)
William Munoz: 26(BL), 27(BL)
Tom McHugh: 8(T,C), 10(B), 12(BR), 27(C), 29(BR), 33(C-cut-out,BR), 40(B), 48(CR), 49(TR), 51(TL), 53(BL), 56(T,B), 57(TL,B), 58, 59(T,CR,BR)
Hans Namuth: 59(BL)
Charlie Ott: 18(C)
Marion Patterson: 38(BL)
O. S. Pettingill: 28(BL)
S. Pettingill, Jr.: 35(BL)
Rod Planck: 31(BR), 55(T)
E. Hanumantha Rao: 40(C), 41(T,BL)
Bonnie Rauch: 19(TL)
Mitch Reardon: 44(T)
Gary Retherford: 20(BC)
J. H. Robinson: 14(T,C)
Margot U. Rainer/Okapia: 27(TR)
Leonard Lee Rue III: Title page, 18(BL), 20(BR), 21(CL), 31(TL), 33(BL), 50(BL), 51(TR,CR,B), 55(T)
Len Rue Jr.: 45(T)
St. Meyers/Okapia: 48(T), 50(BR)
Kjell B. Sandved: 37(TL)
H. Schwind/Okapia: 27(BR)
Gregory K. Scott: 24(T), 30(BL)
Douglas R. Shane: 18(BR)
Alvin E. Staffan: 6(BC,BR), 7(B)
Soames Summerhayes: 13(CL)
Karl H. Switak: 14(C)
Norm Thomas: 27(TL)
A. C. Twomey: 32(BL,BC), 55(BL)
M. E. Warren: 49(C,BR)
Stan Wayman: 42(T,BR) 43(BL)
Virginia P. Weinland: 6(BL)
Ralph Wetmore: 19(C)
Jeanne White: 28(CR), 42(BL)